"Jingle" bells was the first song played in space.

****

When the Candy Cane was invented in Germany, it was made into a "J" for Jesus. The red stripes symbolize his blood.

****

Christmas used to be illegal in the U.S. Oklahoma was the last U.S. state to declare Christmas a legal holiday in 1907.

Christmas trees were first used by ancient Egyptians and Romans.

****

More than 400,000 illnesses are caused by spoilt Christmas leftovers.

****

It is a tradition in Japan to eat KFC for Christmas. Orders must be placed two months in advance!

Jingle Bells may be one of the most well-known Christmas songs, but it was originally composed as a Thanksgiving tune.

****

Americans purchase 1.6 billion Christmas cards every year.

****

Santa Claus initially wore clothes that were in green, purple or blue. It was Coca Cola's marketing to dress him up in Red and that stuck!

The tradition of hanging stockings comes from a legend about marriage.

****

Caroling is based on the English custom of wassailing, which was to toast to someone's good health and fortune.

****

Franklin Pierce was the first president who put up an official White House Christmas Tree.

The N.O.R.A.D. Santa Tracker was created due to a child's misunderstanding.

****

The legendary figure of Santa Claus can be traced back to St. Nicholas, a Turkish-born monk who was known for helping the poor and sick.

****

The reason we give presents during Christmas is to symbolize the gifts given to Jesus by the three wise men.

You can send Santa Claus a letter via the Canada Post Mail system.

****

The abbreviation X in "X-mas" is not technically an abbreviation. It actually stands for "Chi", meaning Christ in Greek.

****

There is a Christmas tree in Spain worth $15 million. It is decked with red, white, pink, and black diamonds.

Rudolph the Reindeer was originally a marketing gimmick to encourage children to buy the company's colouring books.

****

Tinsel was invented in Germany and was once made of real silver.

****

In 1980, the highest selling Christmas toy was a Rubik's cube for $1.99. Now, it retails for $10

The Statue of Liberty is officially the largest Christmas gift ever given.

****

The first batch of eggnog originated from medieval Britain's drink "Posset" — a hot milky ale-like drink.

****

The Christmas tree in Trafalgar Square is donated by the people of Norway to London, as token of gratitude for their assistance during WW2.

The Ancient Greeks considered the mistletoe an aphrodisiac.

****

The first Christmas card ever sent fetched a price of almost $30,000 at an auction!

****

In 1914 during World War I, there was a now famous Christmas truce in the trenches between the British and the Germans.

The world's smallest Christmas card is invisible to the human eye.

****

The Christmas wreath is said to represent Jesus' crown of thorns and the red berries the blood he shed.

****

The highest grossing movie about Christmas since 1980 is "How the Grinch Stole Christmas". It pulled in $260,044,825.

Christmas Day boasts the lowest number of relationship breakups.

****

The word "Merry" in Merry Christmas was not always accepted because being merry used to mean slight intoxication.

****

If you gave all the gifts listed in the "Twelve Days of Christmas", it would equal 364 gifts!

Wedding experts say that Christmas Eve is one of the two most popular days of the year to propose.

****

In Ukraine, spiders are considered symbols of good luck at Christmas.

****

A 2010 Facebook study revealed that two weeks before Christmas is the most popular time for break-ups

The largest gingerbread house ever made was as big as a real house!

****

Christmas lights were so expensive that they used to be rented then sold. An electrically lit tree was a status symbol in the early 1900s

****

Nova Scotia is the world's leading exporter of Christmas trees.

There are nearly 750 different versions of the song "Silent Night".

****

Bing Crosby's version of "White Christmas" is the highest-selling single of all time.

****

The biggest gathering of "elves" ever included over 1,700 of Santa's elves.

It only took six weeks for Charles Dickens to write "A Christmas Carol".

****

You can recycle your Christmas trees by donating them to zoos for elephant chow.

****

A law in Britain to this day forbids you from not visiting church on Christmas Day.

Mistletoe translates to "dung on a stick".

****

Christmas came from the words Cristes Maesse meaning "mass of Christ".

****

The first Christmas was said to be celebrated on December 25, 336 A.D. in Rome.

Poinsettias have been a symbol of Christmas for over a century.

****

Christmas trees usually grow for close to 15 years before they become commercially viable.

****

Other names for Christmas from the old times include "Midwinter", "Nativity", and "Yule".

Around 28 Lego sets are sold every second during the Christmas Season.

****

The tallest Christmas tree ever displayed was in Seattle, Washington. It measured a whooping 221 feet tall!

****

Christmas trees were first decorated with fruits, mainly apples, and then candles, and then electric lights beginning 1895.

In the United States, the day immediately after Christmas is called the National Candy Cane Day.

****

Black Friday is not the busiest shopping day of the year. The two days before Christmas are.

****

Germany is credited with starting the Christmas tree tradition.

There are two islands in the world that are named "Christmas" — one is in the Pacific Ocean, and the other is in the Indian Ocean.

****

The Yule log dates back to a holiday tradition from the Iron Age.

****

1 in 3 men wait until Christmas Eve to do their shopping.

The largest floating Christmas tree in the world — at 278 feet tall — is in Rio de Janeiro, Brazil.

****

A handwritten copy of 'Twas the night Before Christmas was sold for $280,000.

****

Visa cards are used 6,000 times every minute during the Christmas season.

The tallest living Christmas tree is believed to be the 122-foot, 91-year old Douglas fir in Woodinville, Washington.

****

The biggest display of Christmas lights ever was made in Australia.

****

Mariah Carey wrote "All I Want for Christmas is You" in 15 minutes!

Tens of thousands of people go to the ER each year with decorating-related injuries.

****

The top six Christmas tree-producing U.S. States are Oregon, North Carolina, Pennsylvania, Michigan, Washington, and Wisconsin.

****

The United States issued its first Christmas postage stamp in 1962.

A Santa's Village is open 365 days a year in Canada!

****

The first Christmas celebrated on American Land was in 1539 in Florida. There were no trees or presents, just a religious mass.

****

In Guatemala, adults do not exchange Christmas gifts until New Year's Day.

Santa Claus delivering presents come from Holland's celebration of St. Nicholas' feast day on December 6.

****

Christmas lights were invented in 1882 by Edward Johnson.

****

The Charles W. Howard Santa Claus School in Midland, MI hosts 130 Santas each year where they gather and learn about Santa etiquette.

The period from December 25- January 5 is referred to as "Christmastide" or "Twelve Holy Days".

****

King William I of England was crowned on Christmas Day in the year 1066.

****

In order for Santo to visit all the homes on Christmas eve, he would have to visit 822 homes each second.

In Hawaii, Santa is known as "Kanakaloka".

****

Rudolph almost didn't have a red nose, as it was a sign of chronic alcoholism at that time.

****

Between 1640 and 1958, the Parliament of Scotland officially abolished the observance of Christmas.

Before turkey, the traditional Christmas meal in England was a pig's head and mustard.

****

The world's biggest snowman ever was 113 feet tall and was built in Maine.

****

In the U.K. only, 2.4 billion pounds is spent on uneaten, discarded food, and unwanted gifts according to a survey.

Each year, around 10 million turkeys were consumed in the United Kingdom during the Christmas season.

****

The most number of lights lit on simultaneously on a Christmas tree is 194,672.

****

The song "We Wish You a Merry Christmas" originally was sung by servants to demand alcoholic drinks from their masters.

The favorite festive pudding, the Christmas pudding, was initially a soup made with raisins and wine!

****

The star of Bethlehem that guided the wise men is believed to be a comet or the planet Uranus.

****

The first Christmas crackers were made in London in 1847 by Tom Smith.

The term "Boxing Day" is supposed to come from the money raised for the poor in church alms-boxes.

****

The Beatles had Christmas number ones in 1963, '65, and '67, giving them the record for the most Christmas number ones!

****

The gold chocolate coins we receive at Christmas are to represent the gold St. Nicholas gave to the poor.

An estimated 1 of 3 people worldwide celebrate Christmas.

****

Home Alone is one of the most-watched movies during Christmas.

****

Norwegian scientists have hypothesized that Rudolph's red nose is probably due to a parasitic infection of his respiratory system.

Czech Republicans believe a table at Christmas must be made of even numbers otherwise the one without a partner will die.

****

The Germans made the first artificial Christmas trees out of dyed goose feathers.

****

The majority of Sweden's population watches Donald Duck cartoons every Christmas Eve.

Every year, more than 3 billion Christmas cards are sent in the United States alone!

****

Many parts of the Christmas tree can actually be eaten, with the needles being a good source of Vitamin C!

****

Eggnog apparently derives from "egg grog", which means an egg and rum drink.

The "true love" mentioned in the "Twelve Days of Christmas" does not refer to a romantic couple, but the Catholic Church's code for God.

****

The very first Christmas in England took place in York in 521 A.D.

****

A Yule log is literally a giant log that is burnt during the 12 days of Christmas.

In 350 A.D., Pope Julius I, bishop of Rome, proclaimed December 25 the official celebration date for the birthday of Christ.

****

St. Nicholas was originally a stern, harsh man holding a birch branch who symbolized discipline.

****

In Icelandic folklore, the Yule Cat will eat anyone who does not receive new clothes by Christmas Eve.

The traditional three colors of Christmas are green, red, and gold.

****

Contrary to popular belief, suicide rates during the Christmas holidays are low. The highest rates are during the spring.

****

In 1972, the Peruvian government banned Santa Claus from appearing on radio and television.

Many European countries believed that spirits, both good and evil, were active during the Twelve Days of Christmas.

****

Christmas was not declared an official holiday in the United States until 26 June 1870.

****

Streets are closed on Christmas Eve in Caracas, Venezuela so people can roller skate to church.

Reindeer antlers grow at a rate of more than an inch a day, making them the fastest growing tissue of any mammal.

****

Each year, there are approximately 20,000 "rent-a-Santa" across the United States.

****

The song "Silent Night" has been translated to more languages than any other holiday tune.

In the 1950s, Boston church leaders tried to ban the song "I Saw Mommy Kissing Santa Claus" as it supposedly promoted physical intimacy.

****

Bolivians celebrate Misa del Gallo or "Mass of the Rooster" on Christmas Eve. Some people actually bring roosters.

****

Christmas hats, or paper crowns, are only worn in Britain during Christmas.

What do Isaac Newton, Little Richard, and Humphrey Bogart all have in common? They were all born on Christmas Day!

****

Alabama was the first state in the United States to officially recognize Christmas in 1836.

****

Christmas trees are grown across all states in the United States.

In Maria Carey's "All I Want for Christmas Is You", Santa Claus is played by Mariah's then-husband Tommy Mottola.

****

During the Nazi era, Hitler tried to turn Christmas into a non-religious holiday celebrating Hitler.

****

The Christmas Eve meal is not served in Hungary until a twinkling star is seen in the sky.

In 2013, the record for the fastest time to decorate a Christmas tree was set by Sharon Juantuah. It took her only 36.89 seconds!

****

In mid-1400's, while Christmas was banned, mince pies were also outlawed.

****

Christmas tinsel was initially made of lead until the U.S. government persuaded makers to change it to plastic

Harper Lee's friends gave her a year's wages for Christmas in 1956. She took the next year off and wrote "To Kill a Mocking Bird".

****

In 1901, President Roosevelt banned Christmas trees in the White House.

****

In Poland, spiders are common Christmas tree decorations because legend has it that a spider wove a blanket for baby Jesus.

Ancient peoples, such as the Druids, considered mistletoe sacred because it remains green and bears fruit during the winter, when all the other plants appear to die.

****

The candy cane originated 250 years ago in Germany as straight white sticks.

****

The Viking god Odin is one precursor to the modern Santa Claus.

There are approximately 21,000 Christmas tree farms in the United States. In 2008, nearly 45 million trees were planted.

****

The first printed reference to a Christmas tree was in 1531 in Germany.

****

Originally, mince pies were actually filled with meat and were oval to represent Jesus' manger.

In Germany, Heiligabend, or Christmas Eve, is said to be a magical time when the pure in heart can hear animals talking.

****

Christmas purchases account for 1/6 of all retail sales in the United States.

****

"Millionaires Crackers" are Christmas crackers that contain a solid silver box with a piece of jewelry inside.

There is a debate that we actually give gifts at Christmas to commemorate the Pagan tradition of gifting the gods, not the three magi

****

Assuming Rudolph was in front, there are 40,320 ways to rearrange the other reindeers.

****

The earliest Christmas tree decorations were apples.

In the United States, dried Christmas trees cause an estimated 100 fires, resulting in about 10 deaths and 15.7 million in property damage.

****

Turkeys aren't just for Christmas. June is National Turkey Lover's Month.

****

The first decorated Christmas tree was supposedly in 1510 in Latvia.

Calennig is a welsh tradition, like caroling, where children would go round houses singing with an ornate apple.

****

Long before there were Christmas trees, the pagans revered evergreens as symbols of eternal life and rebirth.

****

Turkey replaced the swan on the Christmas menu of the Royals in 1851.

In Scandinavia, the holly is known as Christ Thorn.

****

The city of Riga, Latvia holds the claim as home to history's first decorated Christmas tree, back in 1510.

****

One superstition regarding Christmas pudding is that it shouldn't have more than 13 ingredients to represent Jesus and his disciples.

Some English towns have a Christmas Eve tradition of ringing the Church bells near midnight to announce the supposed Devil's demise.

****

The Christmas carol "Silent Night" originated in Austria.

****

The traditional Christmas Eve meal in Armenia is a portion of fried fish, some lettuce, and spinach.

In 2013, 1.7 million people sent Santa letters, which is the highest percentage of over 8 million letters sent worldwide.

****

The Christmas carol "Silent Night" originated in Austria.

****

In Peru, December 24th, which is known as La Noche Buena ("the Good Night"), is the main day for celebrations.

In spite of Ethiopia's Christian heritage, Christmas is not an important holiday there.

****

On Christmas Day 2011, there were 6.8 million iOS and Android devices activated.

****

People in Iceland will often exchange books on Christmas Eve, then spend the rest of the night reading them and eating chocolate.

On Christmas Day, tradition allows Lebanese children to go up to any adult and say, "Editi 'aleik!" ("You have a gift for me!").

****

In the US, there are 2 places known as Santa Claus and Santa, they are in Indiana and Idaho respectively.

****

Fruitcake originated in ancient Egypt, where it was considered essential for the afterlife.

Syrian children receive gifts from one of the wise men's camels, purported to be the youngest and smallest in the caravan.

****

Since 1991, real Christmas tree sales have plummeted below that of artificial trees.

****

Greenland's traditional Christmas dish, kiviak, takes a full seven months to prepare.

There are 12 courses in the traditional Ukrainian Christmas Eve supper, each of them dedicated to one of Christ's apostles.

****

In China, Santa is known as "Sheng dan lao ren" which means old Christmas man in Chinese.

****

In Ghana, many people observe a traditional folk libation ritual at Christmas time.

In UK churches, the largest church bell is rang an hour before midnight, at midnight all others are rang in celebration.

****

In Greek culture, kissing under the mistletoe was considered an unspoken promise to marry.

****

"O Christmas Tree", also known as "O, Tannenbaum", is based on a traditional German folk song.

"O Come, All Ye Faithful," originally written in Latin in the 17th century, has been attributed to King John IV of Portugal.

****

Supposedly, the Christmas pickle is to be the last ornament on the tree.

****

Native to Mexico, the poinsettia was originally cultivated by the Aztecs, who called it "Cuetlaxochitl".

Norwegians pay only 50% of their usual tax in November, so everyone has more money for Christmas.

****

Eating Chinese food for Christmas is a tradition for many Jewish-Americans.

****

New Zealand bans all television advertising on Christmas Day.

In ancient Egypt and Rome, people hung evergreens around their homes to symbolise fertility and a talisman against evil spirits.

****

An old British law states that everyone is required to attend church on Christmas Day and that they must go on foot.

****

The Christmas Story is in the New Testament of the Holy Bible.

The largest old Christmas market in Europe is the Christkindlesmarkt in Nuremberg, Germany.

****

The song "Jingle Bells" was originally "One Horse Open Sleigh"

****

Queen Elizabeth has made the annual Christmas broadcast since 1952, following in her father's footsteps.

Every December, locals in South Africa feast on a seasonal delicacy– the deep-fried caterpillars of Emperor Moths.

****

"Good Christian Men, Rejoice" is one of the world's oldest traditional Christmas songs, with roots stretching back to the Middle Ages.

****

The tradition of kissing under the mistletoe may come from Norse mythology.

An odd tradition in Catalonia involves a creature called caga tió, or "defecating log." Families dress a log in a hat and place it on the table throughout December.

****

"Carol of the Bells" was based on a Ukrainian folk chant "Shchedryk" or "little swallow" in English.

****

A Giant Lantern Festival is held each year for Christmas in the Philippines.

Apples' shape inspired the round glass Christmas ornaments.

****

1 in 3 Jews in the United States put up a Christmas tree in their home during the holiday season, a survey found.

****

In some European countries, children are given gifts on December 6th rather than on Christmas Day.

About 200 Christmas trees catch fire every year in the United States.

****

Legend has it that Christmas stockings had a backstory featuring three poor sisters.

****

The United Kingdom could fill 57 Olympic swimming pools with the Beer it drinks over Christmas.

The sixth-century Christian Council of Braga banned home decorations due to their pagan associations.

****

Christmas tree decorations in the 1990s included edible food.

****

The Advent wreath began in Germany as a Lutheran tradition, but eventually spread to other Christian denominations.

The first plastic Christmas trees were produced by a toilet brush manufacturer. They used the same bristles and dyed them green.

****

In Japan, Christmas Eve is a time to eat strawberry shortcake and fried chicken.

****

Though only 2% of the nation's population is Christian, Christmas is a national holiday in India.

One of Sweden's more unique Christmas traditions is a Yule goat made of straw, who is believed to help guard the Christmas tree.

****

In Guatemala's villages, local men in devil costumes appear on the streets and chase children during the first week of Advent.

****

Silver aluminum trees rose to fame in mid-1960.

Canada Post assigned Santa the postal code of H0H 0H0 in 1982.

****

"How The Grinch Stole Christmas" almost did not become a movie due to a lack of positive response to calls for sponsorships from candy companies and breakfast foods.

****

Jim Carrey's The Grinch makeup took 3 hours a day to complete.

Tim Burton wrote the poem "The Nightmare Before Christmas" while working at Disney in 1982.

****

Before going big as a TV special, "Frosty The Snowman" was a hit song first.

****

In Estonia, people believed that the first visitor on Christmas, called the "first-footer," would determine the household's luck.

On December 23rd, local Mexican competitors carve nativity scenes into large radishes as part of the annual "The Night of the Radishes".

****

Olden English folk tales have it that the Devil fell when Jesus was born.

****

The most common Christmas gift is a new outfit for wearing to church.

In Costa Rica, the Christmas flower is the orchid.

****

In Austria, farmers traditionally chalk the initials of the Three Wise Men on the archway above stable doors.

****

The Canadian province of Nova Scotia leads the world in exporting three things: lobster, wild blueberries, and Christmas trees.

In January of 2003, after a decree of authorization by President Hosni Mubarak, Christmas was observed as a national holiday in Egypt.

****

Grover Cleveland was the first U.S. president to have a Christmas tree decked out in electric bulbs.

****

In 2015, the full moon fell on Christmas Day for the first time in 38 years.

In Iceland there are 13 Santas, each leaving a gift for children. They come down from the mountain one by one, starting on December 12.

****

In Greece, Italy, Spain and Germany, workers receive a Christmas bonus of one month's salary by law.

****

Christmas lights weren't safe for outdoor use until the 1920s.

A man in Canberra, Australia holds the record for "Most Lights on an Artificial Tree".

****

December 25th is a public holiday for Christmas in Bangladesh even though only about 0.3% of the population are Christians.

****

Residents of Aurora, Illinois face a fine of $50 if they do not take their lights down by February 25.

Christmas in Chile is very warm as it's in the middle of summer!

****

Every year, over 20 million pounds of holiday lights arrive in Shijiao, China, the Christmas tree lights recycling capital of the world.

****

In Brazil, Santa Claus is called *Papai Noel* & *Bom Velhinho* or Good Old Man.

The Midnight Mass service is very popular in Hungary. Most people go to Church after their Christmas meal.

****

In Hong Kong, poinsettias, Christmas lights, and Nativity scenes decorate homes, churches and public places.

****

There is a town in India called Santa Claus.

Washington Irving created the image of Santa's sleigh. His popular stories spawned a Christmas revival in America.

****

The puritan pilgrims renounced Christmas, from 1659 to 1682; it was actually a crime to celebrate!

****

Christmas was banned in Cuba from 1969 until 1998.

The fruits in Jamaica's Christmas cake are soaked in red wine and white rum for months before the holidays.

****

In Estonia, it's traditional for the whole family to take a sauna together on Christmas Eve before church.

****

Every December 7, Guatemalans take part in La quema del diablo, or burning the devil.

In Haiti, children place their newly cleaned shoes filled with straw under the tree on the porch on Christmas Eve.

****

In Eastern European legend, Frau Perchta or the Christmas witch, has two faces - the nice for the good children, and scary for the naughty ones.

****

Many people in the Philippines stay awake all night into Christmas Day!

In Portugal, the people set places in the Christmas morning feast for the souls of the dead.

****

Christmas in Ukraine is celebrated on the 7th of January because they use the old "Julian Calendar" for their church festivals.

****

A special Christmas food in Madagascar are fresh lychees.

In Czech Republic, it is believed that if you throw your shoe over your shoulder on Christmas Day, it can tell if you'll be married that year or not. If the shoe lands pointing at the door, you're gonna get hitched. If not, you're out of luck.

****

Printed in Great Britain
by Amazon